Tomáš Míček

FRIESIAN HORSES

Text by
Dr. Hans-Jörg Schrenk

D1621701

SUNBURST BOOKS

The Friesian stallion, Danilo, trots imposingly across the meadow, making it clear, through his arched neck and erect tail, that this is his territory.

Friesians are always assured of the interest and admiration of horse-lovers, whether they are on parade carrying riders in historical costume, in a classical English team pulling a carriage or harnessed to the traditional "Friesensjees." These black beauties of Friesland with their long, thick manes and silky coats awaken nostalgic memories of times gone by, especially of the Baroque era of mounted displays, when they were used primarily for parades and to demonstrate complicated dressage movements. Tomáš Míček has photographed these attractive black horses in situations where they are not subject to rider or coachman, free from the constraints of saddle or harness, out in the paddocks and meadows.

Two young stallions in a paddock at the Amtmannscherf Stud, owned by Bernd Reisgies.

Horses have been bred in Friesland for over 2,000 years. The horses bred there in the past were certainly the ancestors of today's Friesian horses, influenced to a great extent by cross-breeding with Andalusian horses in the 16th and 17th centuries, at the time of the Spanish occupation of the Netherlands. The Friesians have inherited the strong, Baroque neck, long mane and high-stepping gait of the Andalusian horses. Around this time the Friesian horses were gaining a reputation not only as ideal dressage - or "haute école" - horses, but also as war steeds. Already, in the 17th century, there were strict rules for breeding Friesians and the Friesian race flourished. However around the middle of the last century, the Friesians began to lose the value with which they had formerly been endowed. They no longer fulfilled the buyers' requirements for heavy horses to work the land, and therefore it seemed as if the Friesian breed was doomed to die out.

Portrait of the stallion, Doeke, owned by Eva Natter.

Family group: three Friesian mares with their foals in the paddock at the Amtmannscherf Stud

The stallion, Danilo. The long, flowing mane, the thick tail and the glossy coat are all typical features of the Friesian horse.

The mares and foals gaze at the camera. The foals' coats are still tinged with brown and will gradually turn a glossy black as they get older.

Spacious paddocks and meadowland are required to breed healthy foals.

By growing up in a herd, the horses learn how to get along with each other and to respect the herd hierarchy.

In 1878 a group of Friesian breeders got together and formed a studbook society with the aim of preventing the old Friesian race from dying out. In the original studbook of this society there were 8 Friesian stallions and 10 mares. By 1896 the stock had grown to 133 mares and 7 stallions. In 1913 however the breed had reached another low point, with only 3 remaining stallions. To save the race, the friends of the Friesians formed an association which was to take over the responsibilities of breeding, of maintaining the number of stud stallions and of monitoring the quality of the horses. Nowadays, as a result, the Friesians are a popular leisure horse, well suited to both riding and driving in harness. Many breeding areas throughout the world have been added to the original one in Friesland. In particular there are a large number of studs in the USA and Australia. In Germany there is a union of Friesian breeders which continues to attract many new members.

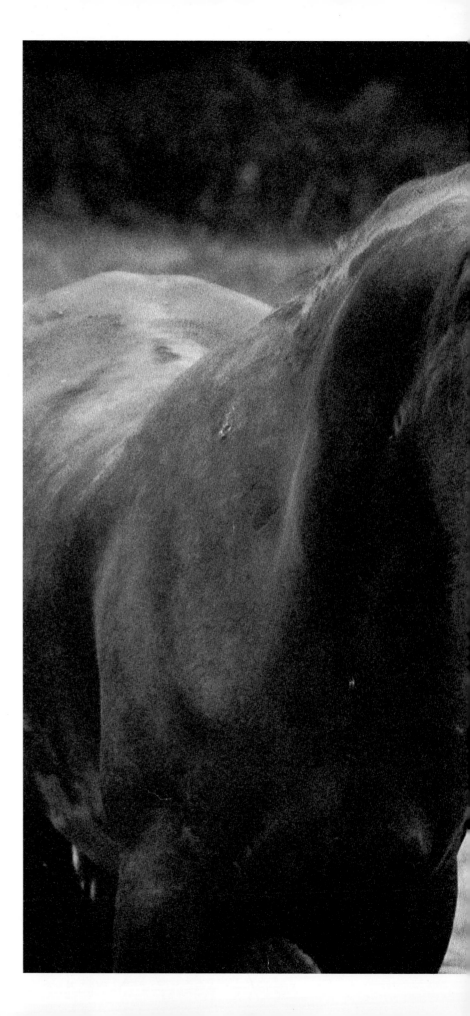

Two of Hans-Günther Fröhlich's mares in Krefeld. When horses are kept in herds, friendships often grow between two animals which can last for years. They usually stand close to one another when they are resting or dozing, take care of each other's coat and eat together.

This foal is warily edging closer to an unknown mare, until he can get to know her smell. In the first few days of their life, foals do not dare to stray far from their mothers, and it is only when they are a few weeks old that they will roam further afield and approach unknown mares.

But the foal always returns to his mother for a drink of milk. At first they feed every half hour, then later every hour, until they are separated from their mother at the age of six to eight months.

This stallion clearly demonstrates the high knee action which the Friesians inherited from their Andalusian ancestors.

On the following pages: Young stallions from the Amtmannscherf Stud. Horses have a certain behaviour pattern, in which they alternate activities such as eating or playing with rest periods. However during these rest times, the animals very rarely fall into a deep sleep. Most of the time they just doze, like the three overleaf.

This mare surveys her surroundings, her ears pricked forward towards something which has caught her attention.

Games are always interrupted by breaks, either to graze or just to have a
breather before they resume play.

The wide brow and long, silky forelock are distinguishing features of the Friesian. This is the stud stallion, Douwe.

The stallion, Doeke, sniffs in vain at a gelding.

The gelding remains undisturbed by the stallion, despite the latter's impressive stature and the blow from his foreleg.

Friesian stallions which are to be used for breeding have to meet the very strict specifications stipulated by the breeders' union. At the age of three they must stand at least 1,58 metres high. If they fulfil this requirement, then they are taken to the stallion examination establishment at Ermelo, where they undergo various performance tests, including their suitability for both riding and driving. The authorities at this establishment also judge the character and training capacity of the horse. However, even if the stallion succeeds in passing all these tests, only a provisional breeding licence will be issued, valid for just one year. At the end of this year, the stallion's offspring will be examined, and if the foals appear to have inherited good genes, then the stallion is granted a licence for breeding which is valid for a few years. The goal of Friesian breeders is to rear a strong horse, with an elegant, arched neck, a broad chest, a slightly divided croup and muscular hind quarters. Equally important are the long mane, thick tail and glossy coat. Today's thoroughbred Friesians are completely black - they are not allowed to have any white spots, not even a small white star between their eyes.

This struggle between the two stallions looks more dangerous than it is - the fact that the ears of both horses are pointing forwards indicates that this is not a serious fight.

One of the stallions draws himself up into a "levade," while the other one
tries to bite his chest.

Then the other stallion also rears up on his hindquarters to evade the blows of his opponent.

In between games, the horses always have short pauses to catch their breath. Here each of the two stallions is waiting to see if the other one is going to resume the playful fight.

There are three different types of Friesian. The most heavily built and stocky draught-horse type has very pronounced joints and is well-muscled overall. This type is not only an ideal carriage horse, but is also suited to heavy agricultural work. It can be distinguished from similar coldbloods by its high knee action and energetic gait. The mid-weight type of Friesian represents the ideal goal for most breeders. This type has a relatively small head, a glossy coat, a wide chest and high, arched neck, with well defined joints. This horse is ideal for both carriage driving and riding. The final type of Friesian is lighter with longer legs. It is very fast and fleet of foot, making it the ideal horse for competitive sports, as demonstrated by the former winner of the carriage-and-four world championship, Tjeerd Velstra.

Yet again the two opponents rear up and their forelegs lock together like wrestlers.

Whilst one of the two fighters turns away wearily and starts to graze, the other flings up his head and flares his nostrils, probably picking up the scent of a mare nearby.

The clear eye of the stud stallion, Douwe, gazes at the observer.

Portrait of the stallion, Franke, owned by Dannefelser.

Two mares grooming each other. This skin care routine usually takes place when the horses are resting in the middle of the day.

A Friesian head in profile. The refined, elegant head distinguishes the Friesians very clearly from the coldbloods with which they are sometimes confused.

Rolling is also part of the horses' skin care routine. They usually seek out dry spots and always go back to the same place to roll if possible.

A final look at the beauty of the Friesian, with flowing mane and tail and boundless strength and energy.